The Armada Book
of Jokes and Riddles

This Armada book belongs to:

_____

_____

_____

Born in Cornwall, Jonathan Clements has in his lifetime been a gravedigger, Admiralty chart-compiler, dustman, artist, actor, roadsweeper, milkman, poet, greengrocer, life-saver, photographer, advertising copywriter, footballer, singer – and, in all, had about two hundred jobs before he turned to writing. When he isn't writing children's books (and this is his sixth), he writes for magazines and throws Frisbees high in the air. His next project is to write a history of pickled onions, or a collection of mind-bending insults. Jonathan Clements lives on Salisbury Plain in Wiltshire, and owns a rusty bicycle named Hortense.

Also by Jonathan Clements

in the same series

The Armada Book
of Jokes and Riddles

Compiled by Jonathan Clements
with drawings by Roger Smith

AN ARMADA ORIGINAL

An Armada Original

This edition first published in 1974
by Fontana Paperbacks,
14 St James's Place, London, SW1A 1PF
This Impression 1978

Printed in Great Britain by
William Collins Sons & Co. Ltd., Glasgow

Contents

Jokes and Riddles to Make People Turn Green

(And an Assortment of Other Sickly Colours)

These are the jokes and riddles that are so earth-shaking that they're liable to make even your best friend turn green with envy – or green at the stomach. In fact, *all* the jokes and riddles in this book have this magic power, depending on whom you tell them to. Using them whenever and wherever you can, will show the world at large that you have a great sense of daring, and possess tremendous courage. (You must do, or you wouldn't have the cheek to tell them out loud!)

Whatever you do, don't tell these jokes and riddles to your teacher, or to any of your wealthy relations – especially if it's near your birthday.

Why is a peacock like the number nine?
Because it would be nought without its tail.

What did one loom say to the other loom?
Let's spin a good yarn.

When is a boy on a bicycle not a boy on a bicycle?
When he turns into a street.

1ST MAN: That's a bad cut you've got on your forehead. How on earth did you get it?
2ND MAN: I bit myself.
1ST MAN: *What!* How could you bite yourself on your forehead?
2ND MAN: I stood on a chair.

PATIENT: I've got water on the knee. What shall I do?
DOCTOR: Wear wellington boots.

LADY CARRUTHERS: Now, Kathleen, remember that we have breakfast *sharp* at 8 o'clock each morning.
NEW MAID: Very good, my lady. And if I'm not up, you just go ahead without me!

What did the chimney sweep say when he was asked if he liked his work?
It soots me.

The Council foreman was very angry when he got a demand for more shovels from his gang of labourers.

'You have enough,' he said. 'And if you do run short – lean on each other!'

How do you make a gardener angry?
Plant a foot in his seed bed.

What carries hundreds of needles but never sews?
A porcupine.

What did one earwig say to the other earwig when they were brushed off the wardrobe?
Erewig-go again.

HOLIDAYMAKER: Does the water *always* come through the roof like this?

LANDLADY: Oh no, sir. Only when it rains.

What book makes light reading?
A match-book.

What runs around the house but never moves an inch?
A fence.

Why is a spinning-top like a kind person?
Because they both do many a good turn.

When did Adam and Eve stop playing games?
When they had lost their pair o' dice (paradise).

Why did the match box?
Because it saw the wood fence.

When are bees in the money?
When they cell (sell) their honey.

MAN: If you really are a police officer, then why on earth are you wearing that red and yellow patterned suit?
CONSTABLE: Just a routine check, sir.

Where would you take your parrot if he needed spectacles?
To the Bird's-Eye shop.

What is so unusual about money?
You have to make it first before you can make it last.

What gun is like the earth?
A revolver.

What does a farmer have in common with a dentist?
They both deal with many acres (achers).

The school was going to have a boxing team, and many boys tried to get into the team. Some were good, and some were terrible. One of the worst, after trying unsuccessfully to land a punch for a few rounds, went over to the coach.

'Have I done my opponent any damage?' he asked.

'No,' said the coach. 'But keep on swinging – the draught may give him a cold.'

PATIENT: I have a very peculiar complaint, Doctor.
DOCTOR: Eh? What is it?
PATIENT: Well, I keep thinking there are two of me.
DOCTOR: Eh? Would you repeat that? And this time, don't both speak at once!

Why was the cricket team given cigarette lighters?
Because they had lost all their matches.

What escaped when the house burned down?
The door bolted, the chimney flue (flew), and the tap ran.

If it took eight men eight hours to build a brick wall, how many hours would it take four men to build it?
None, because the eight men have already done the work.

Why is a big city like a person who boasts?
They are both filled with tall storeys (stories).

What is the brightest day
of the week?
Sun-day.

What can you put in the 'fridge that will stay hot?
Mustard.

What is the difference between a sheep and a dog?
One carries the fleece, while the other carries the fleas.

IRONMONGER: Can I help you, sir?
CUSTOMER: I'd like a mousetrap – and hurry, I've a bus
to catch.
IRONMONGER: Sorry, sir – we don't make them that
big!

ELEPHANT: A pint of beer, please.

BARMAN (*surprised*): Very well . . . That'll be fifty pence.

ELEPHANT: Thank you.

BARMAN: I hope you don't mind my mentioning it, but we don't get many elephants drinking in this pub.

ELEPHANT: I'm not surprised, with beer at fifty pence a pint!

1ST CANNIBAL: Oh, I have such a dreadful pain in my stomach.

2ND CANNIBAL: Who have you been eating?

1ST CANNIBAL: A Franciscan missionary.

2ND CANNIBAL: How did you cook him?

1ST CANNIBAL: I boiled him.

2ND CANNIBAL: Ah, that's why you feel bad. You should never boil Franciscans. They're Friars.

FOREMAN: How would you like to join the work's football team?

NEW WORKER: I'm sorry. I'd like to oblige, but I know nothing at all about football.

FOREMAN: Oh, that doesn't matter. We need a referee!

What holds five dozen keys but never opens a door?
A piano.

What did the cat think when the dog caught him by the tail?
Well, that's the end of me.

What is a good job to have in the winter?
Selling newspapers – each copy sold increases circulation.

Why was the lemon sour?
Because it was pipped by the orange.

TEACHER: Where was the Magna Carta signed?
BOY: At the bottom.

Who make the best letter-writers?
Anglers, because they often drop a line.

What is an uncommon noun?
A pair of trousers – they are singular at the top, and plural at the bottom.

What did the policeman shout to the deaf motorist?
Don't worry – you'll get your hearing in the morning!

ART TEACHER: Why is your canvas blank? You were supposed to have painted a picture!

STUDENT: This is a picture of a cow grazing.

ART TEACHER: Indeed – where is the grass?

STUDENT: The cow has eaten it.

ART TEACHER: But where is the cow?

STUDENT: Well, you don't think she would stay there after eating all the grass, do you?

What did the sole of one shoe say to the other sole?
Beware! There are two heels following us!

Why is a wild pony like an egg?
Both must be broken before they can be used.

'Coffee, without cream,' ordered a guest in a hotel.

'Certainly, sir,' said the waitress. She went to the kitchens, returning five minutes later, empty-handed and apologetic. 'I'm very sorry, sir. We've run out of cream. Would you mind having your coffee without milk instead?'

What does a magazine have in common with a sick person?
Both appear weakly (weekly).

When is a boat like a heap of snow?
When it comes a-drift.

When is water like a kangaroo?
When it makes a spring.

Torturing Your Enemies
with Laughter

*(So That They Die with a Smile
on Their Faces)*

Now you know how to turn people green, it might come
in handy to know the best way of making your enemies
suffer. In this chapter there are lots of jokes and riddles
that can actually make people scream and dance with
pain. Some of them, told to the right enemies at the right
time (preferably at midnight when there's a full moon)
can make them disappear forever. They'll most likely
demand revenge, and get it by quizzing you with riddles
from one of the other chapters in this book. If this is the
case, and you're the victim of a fiendish riddle-asker, the
best thing to do is curl up in bed with a good supply of
sticky buns and lemonade and read the chapter *Riddles
And Jokes to Comfort Yourself With.*

What animal disturbs you in bed at night?
A night-mare.

What runs through the country without effort?
Roads.

Why did the sun-beam?
Because it saw the sky-lark.

Why is a trumpet good-tempered?
Because it can take a blow from anyone.

In a football match, a team of elephants were beating a team of insects by 22 goals to nil. But in the second half the insects put on a centipede, who scored 35 goals in their 35–22 victory.

'Why on earth didn't you play your centipede from the beginning?' said the captain of the elephants.

'We would have,' said the insect's captain, 'but he takes an hour to get his boots on!'

Why did the boy call his pet dog 'Blacksmith'?
Because every time somebody called, the dog made a bolt for the door.

GIRL: I say, what a lovely coloured cow over there.
BOY: It's a Jersey.
GIRL: Really? I thought it was its skin!

Which side of a round cake is the left side?
The side which isn't eaten.

What is the difference between a dressmaker and a nurse?
One cuts dresses, while the other dresses cuts.

What ship can't sail?
A town-ship.

The sweet old lady was proud of the way she had trained her talking parrot and was showing him off to the vicar.

'If you pull his left leg he says The Lord's Prayer,' she explained. 'And if you pull his right leg he says the 23rd Psalm.'

'Marvellous,' beamed the vicar. 'What if I pull both legs at once?'

'I fall flat on my back, you silly old twit!' replied the parrot.

Why is a fishmonger never generous?
Because his business makes him sell fish (selfish).

What is the best definition of a mermaid?
A deep she-fish.

A gang of thieves attacked Bernard Quince, who put up a tremendous struggle. Finally they pinned him down, but all they could find in his pockets was three pence.

'Why on earth did you put up a fight like that for only three pence?' said the attackers.

'Well,' said Bernard. 'I thought you were after the pound note in my sock.'

Why are goats so easy to fool?
Because they swallow everything.

TEACHER: Tell me, as precisely as possible, all you know about the great English water-colour painters of the eighteenth century.
BOY: They're all dead.

What business will always have success?
Shoemaking, because as soon as one pair is made it is soled (sold).

Why are cooks bullies?
Because they whip the cream and beat the eggs.

What would you expect thirty-five rosebuds to come to?
Flowers.

DUCHESS: Joan, you're getting very slack in your work.
MAID: Oh, ma'am?
DUCHESS: Yes. Look – I can write my name in the dust on this piano.
MAID: Gosh, but it must be grand to have an education!

Why did the lazy man put his watch under the bed?
Because he wanted to sleep over-time.

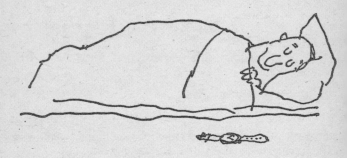

What tradesman is lazy?
A baker, because he is a loafer.

Why is humid weather like a tight shoe?
Because it makes the corn grow.

From what six-letter word can you remove three letters and leave one?
Throne.

Why are plum stones like mile-stones?
They are never found in pears (pairs).

The motorist ran over the farmer's hen, but offered to pay for it.

'I'll give you a pound,' he said to the farmer.

'You'll have to make it two pounds,' said the farmer. 'After all, you've killed two of my best birds.'

'What do you mean?' cried the motorist.

'Well, when the cockerel finds out, he'll die of sheer grief!'

VICAR: My boy – don't you know it's wrong to fish on the Sabbath?

BOY: Oh, I'm not fishing, Reverend. I'm just teaching this little worm how to swim!

What is the difference between a man riding a horse and a dog running beside him?
The man wears trousers and the dog pants.

What has four legs but cannot walk?
An armchair.

Why did the kitchen sink?
Because it saw the tap dance.

DINER: Waiter! My boiled egg is bad!
WAITER: Don't blame me, sir – I only laid the table.

BOY: Father, are slugs nice to eat?
FATHER: Really, Sydney! One doesn't talk about such things at the dinner table. Ask me later.
(*Later:*)
FATHER: Now, Sydney, what was all that about slugs?
BOY: Oh, there was a big one on your dinner plate. But it's gone now.

Why is it against the law to whisper?
Because it is not aloud (allowed).

Why are ships often tied up?
Because they get in so many knots.

How do you make eleven an even number?
Remove the first two letters.

Why did the cotton reel?
Because it saw the silk twist.

The workman on the building site fell from the scaffold and tumbled twenty feet to the ground. His mates gathered around him, and one of them asked:

'Did the fall hurt you, Butler?'

'Oh, no, the fall didn't hurt,' groaned the victim, nursing his aching bones. 'It was the sudden stop!'

DOCTOR: Ah, yes, I can tell you're getting better. You're coughing much more easily this morning.

PATIENT: And so I should be – I've been up all night, practising!

Why should a sailor carry scales?
So he can weigh the anchor.

What did the gas-meter say to the ten-penny piece?
So glad you dropped in; I was just going out.

When is a bad cheese like a top?
When it starts to hum.

Why should a sailor know where King Neptune lives?
Because he has been to see (sea).

When is a cricketer impolite?
When he bowls a maiden over.

1ST MAN: Guess what?
2ND MAN: What?
1ST MAN: I swallowed a pillow in bed last night.
2ND MAN: Good grief! And how do you feel today?
1ST MAN: Oh, a little down in the mouth.

A weedy-looking individual applied for a tree-felling job.
'And where did *you* learn to chop down trees,' the foreman asked him.
'In the Sahara Desert,' said the weed.
'But there are no trees in the Sahara Desert!'
'No, sir. Not *now*.'

PATIENT: Oh, Doctor, you must help me! I'm always being ignored, nobody cares about what I think, nobody notices me –
DOCTOR: Next patient!

When do grapes make news?
When they are in the press.

What looks round but cannot see?
The Earth.

Why are old ladies like fish?
Because they are dear old soles (souls).

FATHER: Nothing to do! Why, when I was your age, I thought nothing of setting out for a ten-mile walk!
SON: Well, I can't say I think much of it myself.

PET-SHOP OWNER: Can I help you?
CUSTOMER: Do you have any dogs going cheap?
PET-SHOP OWNER: Sorry, sir. All our dogs go 'Bow-Wow'!

Jokes and Riddles to Make You Happy

(Even Though They Make Everyone Else Miserable)

When you're sad and feeling forlorn, there's nothing like a good laugh to make you feel bright and good again. Well, perhaps there *is*, but sweets cost money, and you have to queue to get into the pictures. But you don't have to queue to get into this chapter – just wave the book around and the whole house (possibly the entire street) will be deserted in a matter of seconds! Then you'll be free to dip into the laughter-making jokes and riddles, and chortle your head off. If this unfortunate event should happen, immediately consult the chapter titled *Jokes and Riddles to Stick Your Head Back On With.*

What did the arthritis say to the rheumatism?
Let's get out of this joint.

Why didn't the skeleton go to the dance?
Because he had no-body to go with.

Why are boys like a new pair of socks?
Both shrink from washing.

A coalman arrived to make a delivery and was surprised when a parrot shouted the order through the window:
'A ton of coal, please!'
The coalman duly unloaded the sacks, and when he had finished, said to the parrot: 'You're a good talker, Polly.'
'Yes, and I can count too. Fetch the other bag of coal!'

What parts of a river can be eaten?
The source (sauce) and the current (currant).

Why is a children's nursery a good place for dancing?
Because it is a bawl-room (ball-room).

1ST MAN: Which skins make the best slippers?
2ND MAN: I don't know. Which?
1ST MAN: Banana skins!

A holidaymaker saw a man filling bottles with sea-water.
    'How much are they?' he asked.
    'Thirty pence a bottle, sir.'
    The holidaymaker bought two. Later that day he saw the same man on the beach, when the tide had gone out.
    'Gosh,' said the holidaymaker with admiration. 'You *have* been busy! You must have made a fortune!'

What is the most important part of a lion?
The mane (main) part.

What cat is tragic?
A cat-astrophe.

Why will a dustbin collector never accept an invitation?
Because he is a refuse man.

What vegetables should we never put in saucepans?
Leeks.

A woman on a crowded bus was so laden with parcels that, despite searching and searching, she couldn't find her purse to pay her fare.

'Here!' said a man strap-hanging. 'I'll pay her fare.'

The woman started to say how grateful she was.

'Don't mention it,' the man replied. 'You've unbuttoned my braces four times and I was getting nervous!'

Which dog will you find in a ring?
A boxer.

Why cannot two thin people become great friends?
Because they must always remain slight acquaintances.

DOCTOR: Just what seems to be wrong?

PATIENT: I want people to treat me as a normal human being. Everybody makes me out to be some kind of a nut!

DOCTOR: Do you always wear a clothes-peg on your nose?

PATIENT: See what I mean? You're as bad as the rest, you swine!

In a London street market a boastful American picked up a melon and with a scornful laugh asked the stall-keeper:

'Say, is this the biggest apple you can grow around here?'

The stall-keeper looked the American coolly in the eye, and told him: 'Buy that grape or else put it down.'

If you invited a toad to your party what would you sit him on?
A toadstool.

FATHER: Well, son, how are your marks at school?
SON: They're under water.
FATHER: What do you mean 'under water'?
SON: Below 'C' level.

When is it a good time to put money on a horse?
When it is twenty to one.

Why is a sponge cake like the sun?
Because it is light when it rises.

When do you feel like the wheel of a bicycle?
At night when you are tyred (tired).

Why is a cat drinking milk like a racing driver?
Both go on for lap after lap.

What is a waste of time?
Telling a hair-raising story to a bald-headed man.

GIRL: I'd like a ticket for Ouida please.
RAILWAY CLERK: Right . . .
   (*The railway clerk spent an hour searching through his timetables and books in vain. In desperation he turned to the girl*)
RAILWAY CLERK: Tell me something, Miss. Just *where* is Ouida?
GIRL: Oh, she's over there – sucking a stick of liquorice.

Why did Oliver Twist?
Dickens only knows.

What part of a ship is strict?
The stern part.

What did the flour say to the water?
We'll be kneaded to make the dough.

In Ancient Greece the Gods once challenged the Mortals to a football match. The Gods were surprised to see that one of the opposing team was half-man and half-horse.

'Who on earth is that?' asked Jove.

'Ah,' said the Mortal's captain. 'That's our centaur-forward.'

What did one tonsil say to the other?
It's spring again – here comes a swallow.

Why should you never tell a secret to a peacock?
Because they are known to spread tails (tales).

Why did the burglar cut the legs off his bed?
So he could lay low for a while.

The inspector got on the bus and climbed the stairs to the top deck. 'Tickets, please!' he called. He looked very suspiciously at one man's ticket.

'And where did *you* get on?' said the inspector.

'Downstairs, stupid!' said the man.

When is a clock at the top of a staircase dangerous?
When it runs down and strikes one.

What do we all put off until night-time?
Our night-clothes.

What is the definition of a doughnut?
A crazy millionaire.

What letter is a quarter of a yard long?
The letter Y.

BOY: Excuse me, sir, but I don't think I deserve getting 0 per cent on this exam paper.

TEACHER: Neither do I, but it's the lowest mark I can give.

What did one tooth say to the other at the dentist?
Boy – do I feel bored.

Conversation overheard in a music shop:
MOUSE: Have you got a mouse-organ, please?
SHOPKEEPER: Er . . . yes. Here we are. That's funny –
we had a mouse in here earlier today asking for a
mouse-organ.
MOUSE: Oh, that must have been our Monica!

How do you find out the weight of a whale?
Take him to the nearest whaleweigh (railway) station.

What is the difference between a leopard and a comma?
*One has claws at the end of his paws, while the other is a
pause at the end of a clause.*

What did the pig say as the sun grew hotter?
Phew! I'm bakin' (bacon).

What is the world's wealthiest country?
Ireland, because its capital is always Dublin (doublin').

SUNDAY-SCHOOL TEACHER: Now, class, why did Mary
and Joseph take Jesus to Jerusalem with them?
BOY: Because they couldn't get a baby-sitter.

IDIOT: I woke up last night with the feeling that my
watch was gone. So I got out of bed and looked everywhere for it.
FRIEND: And was the watch gone?
IDIOT: No. But it was going.

A bored cat and a very interested-looking cat were watching a tennis match at Wimbledon.

'You seem very interested in tennis,' said the bored cat.

'Oh, it's not that,' replied the other. 'But my father's in the racket.'

The Right Way to Tell Jokes and Riddles

(*Without Perishing in the Process*)

Probably the best way to tell jokes and riddles is to shut yourself in a wardrobe and tell them to yourself. Then at least you'll be safe. But if you insist on torturing your fellow-mortals with these fragments of glittering wit, it's best to follow this list of rules:

1. Tell the jokes and riddles as quickly as possible. With any luck, your victim won't hear you.
2. Always put a hardback book in the seat of your trousers before telling a riddle to a grown-up.
3. Wear a bullet-proof vest. (To bullet-proof an ordinary vest, line it with good-quality steel-plating.)
4. Wear spiked running shoes.
5. Never tell a riddle before a meal. You might go hungry.

What can travel at the speed of sound but has neither legs, wings or an engine?
Your voice.

When is a child not a child?
When it is a little deer (dear).

What did the big flower say
to the little flower?
Hiya, bud.

Why is a cautious man like a screw?
Because his head stops him from going too far.

It was the first time the man had ever tried to ride a horse. He nervously pointed this out to the groom at the riding school.

'Don't you worry about it, sir,' said the groom. 'I'm giving you a horse which has never been ridden before.'

Where do all the sick ships go?
To the dock (doc).

UNCLE: I hear you play football for the school team now.

BOY: Yes, that's right, Uncle.

UNCLE: And what position do you play?

BOY: I'm not quite sure, but I heard the coach saying I was the team's main drawback.

Why couldn't I tell you the tale of the red-hot poker?
Because you couldn't grasp it.

What has two eyes but can't see a thing?
Two needles.

The seaside landlady told the holidaymaker: 'I charge £2 a night. But it's only £1 if you make your own bed.'

'Okay,' said the holidaymaker, 'I'll do that, then.'

Whereupon the landlady promptly handed him a hammer, some nails, and a stack of wood.

MAN: I used to be a tap-dancer.
GIRL: Really? How wonderful!
MAN: Not really – I had to give it up.
GIRL: Why?
MAN: I kept falling in the sink.

Why is a bull in a china shop like a large wave?
They are both breakers.

Which word is always spelt wrongly?
Wrongly.

One of the longest words in the world is antidisestablishmentarianism. How do you spell this?
T-h-i-s.

1ST MAN: My father and Dan Fidget were fighting for twenty years before it came to an end.
2ND MAN: Did they bury the hatchet?
1ST MAN: No. They buried Dan Fidget.

What kind of baby would
thrive on giraffe's milk?
A baby giraffe.

Who hold up trains but are never arrested?
Bridesmaids.

What men are always above board?
Chessmen.

Why did the blue-tail fly?
Because the red-back spider (spied her).

Why is an actress very fortunate?
Because her work is all play.

What is the most shocking city in the world?
Electri-city.

Two cowboys got lost in the desert of Arizona. They were just about to starve to death when one of them shouted:

'Look – food at last! There's a pork-pie tree . . .'

He galloped off, but was back in a few minutes, a cluster of arrows sticking in his hat. 'Shucks, that wasn't a pork-pie tree. It was an am-bush.'

COOK: Elsie! Why have you taken over an hour to fill that salt-cellar?

MAID: I'm sorry, but the holes in the top are so small it's terribly hard to get the stuff in!

If you are given a very difficult problem, which is the best angle to approach it?

A try-angle.

What runs but never walks?

An engine.

Out for his regular early morning stroll, the Bishop saw a little girl trying to reach the knocker of a door.

'Let me, my dear,' said the Bishop, giving the knocker several loud raps.

'That's it,' said the little girl. 'Now run like hell!'

MAN: Good grief – a crab's just bitten my toe!
GIRL: Which one?
MAN: I don't really know. All crabs look alike to me.

When is a hat like a caning?
When it is felt.

What can you look through but not see through?
A book.

Which is the oldest tree of all?
The elder.

Why would you expect a very busy doctor to be good-tempered?
Because he must have lots of patients (patience).

What did the mayonnaise
say to the chef when he took
off the lid?
How dare you – I'm dressing!

What did the kangaroo say when the train ran over his
tail?
It won't be long now.

What makes a light furious?
When it is put out.

JUDGE: Russell! I have a suspicion that you've been up
    before me – am I right?
RUSSELL: Dunno, Judge, what time do you usually get
    up?

Why is a cricket player like a coward?
Because he hits and runs.

Name a band in which there are no musical instruments.
An elastic band.

What does nobody want to have but nobody who has one want to lose?
A bald head.

What did the little hand say to the big hand as they went around the clock?
Meet me in an hour.

The doctor decided to put the very fat Mrs Grosvenor on a strict diet.

'You can have four lettuce leaves,' he said. 'One piece of dry toast, a glass of orange juice and a tomato.'

'Very well, doctor,' said Mrs Grosvenor. 'Do I take them before or after meals?'

What language would you expect to hear from a Bedouin with no teeth?
Gum Arabic.

The city girl was watching the farmer milk the cow.

'Easy, isn't it?' he grinned.

'Seems to be,' said the girl. 'But how do you turn it *on*?'

What is the oldest plant in existence?
Thyme.

A very mean Scotsman once travelled down to Wembley to watch the big international match between Scotland and England. When he returned home, one of his friends asked him:

'Was it a big gate, Jock?'

'It was indeed,' he replied. 'One of the biggest I've ever had to climb over!'

What roof can't you climb on?
The roof of your mouth.

What sea creatures are extremely lazy?
Oysters, because they are always in their beds.

A man bought a diving-suit and helmet, and waded into the sea. Walking about on the ocean bed, he was surprised to see a swimmer flailing about in nothing but a pair of swimming trunks. Extracting a special notebook from his suit, the diver wrote: 'What are you doing down here without a diving-suit and helmet?'

The other man snatched the notebook and wrote: '*Drowning!*'

GIRL: I was ill when the school play was performed. Did it have a happy ending?

BOY: Oh yes. Everybody was happy when it ended.

Jokes and Riddles to Begin the Day With

(If You Don't Mind Ending It a Few Minutes Later)

It was the philosopher Socrates who first said: 'Taking a cold bath is the only healthy way to begin the day.' Which only proves that Socrates was crazy. For the only *civilized* way to greet the new day is to leap brightly out of bed, open the window wide, cast a jolly jest at the world – then leap straight back into bed again. Therefore, the jokes and riddles in this cheerful chapter have been chosen for their intellectual qualities and brevity. Begin the day with one of these and you'll soon find life is much more fun. Especially if upon leaping back into bed you fall asleep again. (Don't try counting riddles instead of sheep if you can't go to sleep, by the way. That's just *asking* for nightmares.)

What did one ear say to the
other ear?
*Between you and me we need
a haircut.*

When did only three vowels exist?
Before U and I were born.

What is the best thing to do when you are run down?
Take the car's number.

A rustic type with straw in his hair handed over a £5 note
at the station booking office.

'Does the next train go to London?' he asked.

'That's right, sir. Change at Tunbridge Wells.'

'I ain't waiting till I gets to Tunbridge Wells!' shouted
the rustic. 'I want my change now!'

MARY: I've discovered a marvellous slimming diet!
JOAN: What's that?
MARY: Eat dripping all the day long.
JOAN: Why dripping?
MARY: Well – constant dripping wears away a stone!

Why is a shop like a yacht?
Because they both have sales (sails).

How should you treat a baby goat?
Like a kid.

Why does a piglet eat most of the time?
To make a hog of himself.

What did the south wind say to the north wind?
Let's play draughts.

What did the roof say when the tornado rushed past?
I'm off.

Conversation overheard at the golf club:
   'Why don't you play with Major Perkins any more?'
   'Well, would *you* play with a man who cheats and tells lies about his score?'
   'Of course not.'
   'Neither will Major Perkins.'

Why can't you fool a snake?
Because he hasn't a leg to pull.

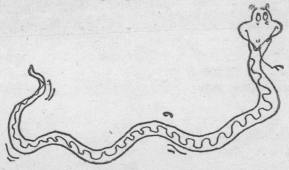

JUDGE: That will be ten pounds or a month in jail.
HENRY: Very well, sir, I'll take the ten pounds!

A preacher was just about to read the first lesson when he noticed Duffield, an ardent football fan, asleep in the front pew. Hoping to wake him, he raised his voice and announced the lesson:

'Ecclesiastes Twelve!'

Duffield awoke with a jump: 'Who on earth were they playing?'

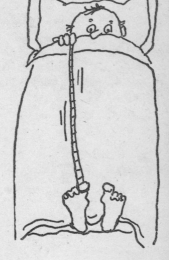

Why would you take a tape measure to bed?
To see how long you slept.

Why did the pound note stamp?
Because the tenpenny bit.

Why was Lady Godiva's horse like a four-quart jug?
It held a gal on (gallon).

FIRST BOY: Lend me twenty pence.
SECOND BOY: I've only got fifteen pence.
FIRST BOY: That's all right. Give me that, and you can owe me five pence.

Two mourners were discussing the recent funeral of their extremely mean friend, Albert Quink:

'Oh, well, that's old Albert laid to rest. They say he left five thousand in his will.'

'Albert never left it. He was taken away from it!'

What is unusual about buying coke?
The buyer generally transfers it to the cellar (seller).

When is a cricketer worried?
When he's stumped.

'What did you think was United's biggest mistake this afternoon?' asked one fan to another after their team had been beaten 7–0.

'Coming out on to the field in the first place,' replied his friend.

WIFE: Harry – wake up!

HUSBAND: What? What's the matter?

WIFE: Harry, I'm *sure* I heard a mouse squeak.

HUSBAND: Well, what do you expect *me* to do – put oil on it?

Why is a pig the most contradictory animal?
Because first you kill it, then you have to cure it.

When is a good time to put corn in your shoes?
When you have pigeon-toes.

ST PETER: How did you get up here?

NEW ARRIVAL: 'Flu.

When is a Scotsman like a donkey?
When he stands on his banks and braes (brays).

When is an eye not an eye?
When an onion makes it water.

COACH: You'd be a good player if it weren't for two things.
FOOTBALLER: What are those?
COACH: Your feet.

Why should everyone feel sorry for a lawnmower?
Because man makes it for lawn (forlorn).

Where would you see the dance of the snowmen?
At the snowball.

Why should you feel sorry for a pelican?
Because he always has a bill facing him.

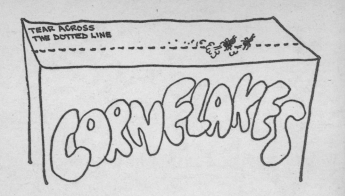

Two little ants were racing as fast as they could across the top of the cereal box.

'Hey!' puffed one ant. 'What are we running so fast for?'

'Can't you *read*?' said the other. 'It says right here: "Tear across the dotted line"!'

What is the keynote to being a gentleman?
B natural.

What did the waiter say when the customer said: 'Hey there!'
Two bales coming, sir.

How do you trap a squirrel?
Hang from a tree and act like a nut.

What did the father ghost say to his son?
Spook only when you are spooken to!

BOY: Quick, help me get a shovel! My brother fell in the mud up to his shoelaces.
GIRL: His shoelaces? Why doesn't he just walk out, then?
BOY: He fell in head first . . .

TEACHER: Did you write this poem yourself?
PUPIL: Every line of it.
TEACHER: Well, I'm glad to meet you, Mr William Shakespeare. I thought you were dead.

What's the best thing to give as a parting gift?
A comb.

Why should a savage dog always be a hungry man's best friend?
Because he's sure to give him a bite.

TEACHER: You're late, Murgatroyd – you should have been here at nine o'clock!
PUPIL: Why, what happened?

What part of England has the most ignorant people?
London, because that is where the population is most dense.

BOY: Just look at that dog chasing its tail.
GIRL: Well, it's just trying to make both ends meet.

What beats a good wife?
A bad-tempered husband.

What is the difference between a boy starting school and an engine driver?
One has a mind to train, while the other has a train to mind.

What letters of the alphabet remind one of the South Pole?
I.C.

Why did the farmer give the pig a collar?
To go with his pig's tie (pig sty).

What did the mouse do when he came home to find the house on fire?
He dived in, dragged his children out, and gave them mouse to mouse resuscitation.

When is a window like a heavenly body?
When it's a skylight.

Jokes and Riddles You Can Eat

(Provided You've a Strong Stomach and a Weak Head)

Few people realise that jokes and riddles make a delicious snack, or even a five-course meal. They *can* be eaten raw, but this is not advisable – unless you've a cast-iron stomach: the resultant indigestion can cause unearthly tremors and blobs before the eyes. Here are a few recipes to try:

ROAST RIDDLE: Tell an awful riddle to your vicar. He will probably send you to Hell, where the central heating is free, and hot enough to roast your riddle to perfection.

JUGGED JOKE: Write a joke on a pancake, using blackcurrant jam instead of ink. Get a friend to do the same. Then tell each other the jokes. The one who laughs loudest wins the pancakes. The other starves.

Why was the robber caught when he hid in the steeple? *Because somebody rang the bells and they tolled (told) on him.*

What has twenty-two yellow legs and two wings? *A Chinese football team.*

Why should you feel sorry about the letter L? *Because it's always in ill-health, and never appears in good spirits.*

Sir Lancelot's horse was killed in a terrible battle. The knight didn't want to give up, so he went in search of another horse. He came to a farm and asked the farmer for a horse.

'I'm afraid I haven't a horse to spare,' said the farmer. 'But I've got a large St Bernard dog you can ride on.'

Sir Lancelot looked at the huge dog and groaned: 'Surely you wouldn't send a knight out on a dog like this?'

What's the hardest thing you come in contact with when you are learning to ride a bike?
The footpath.

In what game do you need to wear ear-plugs?
Tennis, because you can't play without a racket.

A man walked up to a forlorn-looking motorist who'd just crashed his car into a brick wall.
'Have an accident?' he asked.
The motorist groaned: 'No thanks – I've just had one.'

WOMAN: I'll have four nice pork chops, please. And make them lean.
BUTCHER: Certainly, madam. Which way?

SHIPWRECKED GAL: Oh, look – cannibals!
SHIPWRECKED PAL: Come now, don't get in a stew.

Why does a king never have to worry about building expenses?
Because his palaces are always built for a sovereign.

A park-keeper, doing his final rounds, saw a tramp sleeping on a bench. He went over and gave the tramp a sharp dig in the ribs.

'Hey!' cried the park-keeper. 'I'm just going to close the gates.'

'Very well,' said the tramp with a yawn. 'Don't slam them too loud, will you?'

When are you likely to drown in bed?
*When your bed spreads, your pillow slips, and you tumble
into the springs.*

What is the dead centre of London?
The cemetery.

Two flies settled on a coffee cup. Which one lost its
patience first?
The one which flew off the handle.

Why did the deaf woman
ask for the letter A?
Because it made her hear.

CUSTOMS OFFICIAL: And what have you got there?
OLD LADY. A bottle of Holy Water from Lourdes.
   (*The Customs Official opens the bottle and sniffs sus-
piciously.*)
CUSTOMS OFFICIAL: This isn't Holy Water – it's gin!
OLD LADY: Lord bless us. A miracle already!

What Roman numeral can climb a fence?
IV (Ivy).

What do you get after it's been taken?
Your photograph.

Why did the Indians beat the white men to America?
Because they had reservations.

CUSTOMER: Excuse me – is this spray good for mosquitoes?
SHOPKEEPER: Certainly not, it kills 'em stone dead.

The old countryman had been to the city and was advising his brother what to see in London's famous zoo:
'There'll be a sign "To the Elephants" and you'll like them,' he said. 'And there'll be a sign "To the Lions" and they're very interesting. But don't pay any attention to the sign that says "To the Exit". They haven't got one of those. I looked.'

A man bought ninety hens. He placed thirty on the first perch, thirty on the second perch, and the remaining thirty on the top perch. Which hens did he own?
Only the ones on the first perch – because the others were on higher perches (higher purchase).

A nervous tourist peered down from the top of St Paul's Cathedral and asked the guide:
'Do people fall off here often?'
'Oh, no, sir,' said the guide. 'Only once!'

What is peculiar about a
novelist?
*He has tales (tails) coming
from his head.*

What's a good way to make your money go a long way?
Fill your wallet with notes, then take a plane to Timbuctoo.

Why do ships have round portholes?
So the sea water won't hit the passengers square in the eye.

Who created spaghetti?
Somebody using his noodle.

What's the best thing to do before you get off a train?
Get in it.

What's a good way of putting on weight?
Eat a peach, swallow the centre – and you've gained a stone!

BOY: Dad – there's a man at the door with a moustache!
FATHER: Tell him I've already got one.

What's the best thing to do if you feel hungry?
Keep walking until you're fed up.

Do people get fur from a skunk?
Yes, as fur as possible.

If a fly and a flea crawled along a dog's back and the fly overtook the flea, what time would it be in China?
Fly past flea (five past three).

Two's company, three's a crowd – but what is four and five?
Nine.

What does a pretty girl have in common with a hinge?
They both mean something to adore (a door).

The teacher was giving his class a stern lecture about hooliganism at football matches.

'It is very wrong to throw bottles at people,' he said. 'Can anybody tell me why?'

'Yes, sir,' said a small boy. 'There might be tuppence deposit back!'

When is a dog like a camera?
When it snaps.

Where do you find the most fish?
Between the head and the tail.

Where did Noah keep his bees?
In the archives (ark hives).

When is it easy for a convict to escape from jail?
When he finds the walls are built to scale.

Down and down poured the rain in torrents, faster and faster, harder and harder.
   'Oh, it's raining cats and dogs,' said a girl.
   'I know,' said her friend. 'I just stepped in a poodle.'

Why wasn't the skunk allowed into the circus?
Because he only had a scent (cent) and that was a bad one.

Who always considers two heads are better than one?
A barber.

What happened when the lights went out at the local meeting?
The crowd shot their hands up and said: 'Many hands make light work.'

What relation is one step to another?
A step farther (step-father).

A cowboy saw a dog disappear over a cliff one day. What did he remark?
'Doggone!'

What grows larger when it's upside-down?
The number 6.

Why are jockeys like clouds?
They both hold reins (rains).

Donald Tinker was a champion pole-vaulter and was suddenly hit by an attack of pneumonia. The doctor came and took his temperature.

'How high, Doctor?' asked the patient.

'One hundred and five,' said the medical man.

'I see,' said Donald. 'And tell me – what's the record?'

FOOL: A return ticket, please!

RAILWAY CLERK: Where to?

FOOL: Why, back here, of course!

New Uses for Old Jests

(Not to be Confused with Old Vests)

Despite what you may think, jokes and riddles aren't just for making people laugh (or cry). They can perform many valuable social and artistic functions. Out of the thousands of uses jokes and riddles can be put to, here are two instances:

1. *Curing the Sick*
   Many bedridden hospital patients, when being told jokes and riddles, have leapt out of bed – and vanished.

2. *Inspiring Great Inventors*
   When Alexander Graham Bell was asked the riddle, 'Why is a piece of toffee on fire like a telephone?' he replied: 'What's a telephone?' To find out, Bell went ahead and invented the telephone.

   No doubt you can find even wilder uses for the following gags (apart from gagging people with them) . . .

What did the parrot say to
the spaniel?
I'm a cockatoo (cocker, too).

Why are storks seen to lift only one leg?
Because if they lifted both, they would fall over.

Why is it dangerous to rob a bank?
Because it is full of coppers.

The expert Council workmen were watching a new man
from the road-sweeping department, who was busy at
work.

'He's not doing too badly,' said one. 'I think he'll learn
the trade.'

'Don't be too hasty,' growled the other. 'So far he's
only done up-and-down sweeping. Wait till he has to do
a bit of fancy work around a lamp-post.'

Why did the river bend?
Because it saw the water-fall.

What is the untidiest part of a ship?
The officers' mess.

What should you do with a seed, and a stocking with a
hole in it?
Sow (sew) both of them.

How many sides has a jar got?
Two – inside and outside.

When is a boxer like a tramp?
When he's down and out.

TEACHER: Johnson – stop showing off. Do you think you're the teacher of this class?
BOY: No, sir.
TEACHER: Right, then stop behaving like a fool.

How would you address a tailor you didn't know?
Mr So and So (sew and sew).

When is a boy not a boy?
When he turns into a back alley.

Why is the next in line to the king like a cloudy day?
Both are certain to rain (reign).

The short-sighted old lady was looking for the Electricity Board showrooms. By mistake she wandered into the local pet-shop and approached the manager.

'I'd like an infra-red griller,' she said.

The manager looked at her in puzzlement for a minute.

'I'm afraid we haven't got one of those,' he said. 'But I can let you have a nice ultra-violet chimpanzee.'

When is a cow not a cow?
When it is led (lead).

POSTMAN: Whew – I'm exhausted! I've had to walk five miles to your farm with this letter.
FARMER: Why didn't you send it by post?

Have engines got ears?
Yes, engin-eers.

What do banks and trees have in common?
Both have branches everywhere.

PASSENGER: I say, Conductor – do you stop at the
  Savoy Hotel?
CONDUCTOR: What, on *my* wages?

Why is the sun very cruel?
Because it tans so many people.

Mr Jones put on a coat and a hat and went for a walk.
Which arrived back home first?
The hat, because he went on a-head.

Can ten go into two?
Yes – ten toes into two socks.

MATHS TEACHER: Now, if I lay four eggs here, and seven eggs over there, how many eggs will I have altogether?

PUPIL: Well, to tell you the truth, sir, I don't believe you can do it!

What did the hamburger say to the tomato?
That's enough of your sauce.

Why is a ship at sea polite?
Because it always bows to the waves.

MECHANIC: The trouble with your car is simple, madam. The battery's flat.

WOMAN: Oh, dear. What shape should it be, then?

When day breaks, what happens to the pieces?
They go into mourning (morning).

A young man took his girlfriend to a football match for the first time. She was quite bewildered by everything.

GIRL: What's that man doing by that big net?

MAN: He's the goalkeeper. He has to stop the ball going into the net.

GIRL: And how much do they pay him?

MAN: Oh, about £50 a week.

GIRL: Goodness! Surely it would be a lot cheaper to have it boarded up?

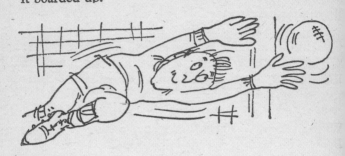

What does the ocean say when it sees the coast?
Nothing. It just waves.

What did Robin Hood say when Little John fired at him?
That was an arrow escape.

What part of a ship can be drunk?
The port side.

Why is a clock unclean?
Because it works twenty-four hours a day, yet never washes its hands.

Why did the kitchen sink?
Because it saw the cellar stair (stare).

What is bought by the yard and worn by the foot?
A carpet.

When is a river bankrupt?
When it breaks its banks.

When is a tap not a tap?
When it is dripping.

Why couldn't the ship's officers play cards?
Because the captain was standing on the deck.

Why is a batsman a coward?
Because he is scared of a duck.

It had been a terrible harvest, and the two farmers were grumbling to each other about it:

'The wheat was so poor,' said one, 'that I had to harvest it with nail scissors.'

The other farmer grimaced. 'That's nothing, Giles. I had to lather my field and shave it.'

Why is a radio set never ever complete?
Because it is always a wire-less.

What tree had the best food?
The pan-try.

DOCTOR: I'm afraid I can't diagnose your complaint. It must be the drink.
PATIENT: Okay – I'll come back when you're sober!

1ST MAN: What breed of dog have you got there?
2ND MAN: It's a boxer.
1ST MAN: Well, it can't be a very good one – just look at its face!

What is it you can lose that nobody else can find for you?
Your temper.

What toe never gets corns?
Mistle-toe.

GIRL: Oh, Ernie – you remind me of the sea.
BOY: You mean wild, restless and romantic?
GIRL: No. You make me sick.

1ST FISHERMAN: Why are you baiting your hooks with razor blades and breadcrumbs?

2ND FISHERMAN: I'm hoping to catch some fish fingers.

Famous Riddles
and Jokes in History

*(That You Won't Find in the
Usual Text-Books)*

Any history teacher will tell you that the history of riddles
and jokes goes way back to the primitive days of cavemen.
(Perhaps that's where they *really* belong.) At the moment,
there is great dispute in the archaeological world regarding
the first riddle ever told. Some experts insist that it was a
neolithic caveman who posed the problem: 'Why did the
brontosaurus cross the ocean?' The trouble is, all he could
really grunt was 'Ug, splot,' so nobody could answer: 'To
get to the other tide.' But throughout the centuries,
riddles and jokes have formed part of the fabric of
civilisation. This chapter features a selection of riddles
attributed to illustrious writers and poets, novelists and
knee surgeons. See if you can guess who wrote the riddles
and jokes. Here's a clue to start with: the first riddle was
(or wasn't) written by William Shakespeare.

Who invented the steam engine?
Watt's-his-name.

What makes men mean?
The letter A.

When is a road angry?
When it is a cross road.

Why did the tin whistle?
Because only a tin can.

The father of a stubborn girl was told by a friend to be more kind to the girl. So he offered to make her something nice to eat.

FATHER: Now, dear, what would you really like?
GIRL: A worm!
FATHER: What . . . Oh, very well, here you are.

GIRL: *You've* got to eat half first.
FATHER: What! Oh, very well . . . Uggh!
GIRL: Oh, Daddy! You've eaten the half *I* wanted. I'll have a boiled egg instead.

What does a kettle suffer with?
Boils.

Where will you always find two trees?
Where there are pear (pair) trees.

WOMAN: Did you save my little boy from drowning?
MAN: Yes, madam, I did.
WOMAN: Well – where's his cap?

Why is a fog like a lost boy?
They are both mist (missed).

Why is the letter A like a flower?
Because the B follows it.

Who was the world's greatest thief?
Atlas, because he held up the whole world.

A lazy man was fishing off the end of the pier when an onlooker fell into the sea. He couldn't swim, and as he threshed about in the water, about to go under for the second time, the fisherman called to him:

'I say, when you go down, do have a look and see if my bait is still on my hook.'

What key plays tricks with
everyone?
A monkey.

LANDLADY: This is a quiet, respectable house. I hope
you haven't brought a record player or a radio with
you?
HOLIDAYMAKER: Oh, no.
LANDLADY: And you don't sing when you have a bath,
or make loud noises getting ready for bed?
HOLIDAYMAKER: Oh, no. One thing, though – I'll be
writing postcards home, and my pen scratches.

When is an artist someone to be feared?
When he draws a gun.

What is above an admiral?
His hat.

Why are tall people the laziest?
Because they are the longest in bed.

What did the tourist write on the postcard from Cuba?
Havana good time. (Having a good time.)

What is the difference between Mount Everest and cod-liver oil?
One is hard to get up and the other is hard to get down.

An idiot telephoned the airport and asked: 'How long does it take to fly to South America?'
    The receptionist answered: 'Just a minute – '
    'Thanks very much,' said the idiot, and hung up.

Why is a beaten boy like a football stand?
They are both in tears (tiers).

PATIENT: I keep imagining I can hear a brass band, Doctor – it's driving me mad!
DOCTOR: Do speak up, Mr Nash. I can't hear a word you're saying for that blasted brass band!

What is the longest word in the English language?
Smiles. Because there is a mile between the first and the last letters.

When is it not sinful to lie?
When it is bedtime.

96

Every morning for years, the little man walked out to his gatepost and poured a mixture of milk, soap powder and rhubarb leaves over it. One day his curious neighbour could stand the suspense no longer, so he went out and asked him why he did it.

'It's to keep the wild elephants away,' explained the little man.

His neighbour laughed. 'But there are no wild elephants around here!'

'You see,' said the little man. 'It really *works*.'

What is the widest rope in the world?
Europe.

A famous surgeon took his suit back to the tailor's and complained: 'This suit is all wrong!'

'What's the matter with it?' asked the tailor.

'I don't know,' said the surgeon. 'It fitted perfectly until I took all the stitches out!'

Why are bridges annoying?
Because they are built over rivers to make people cross.

What flares up when struck on the head?
A match.

What patches never require a needle and thread?
Cabbage patches.

Why did the boy doze off in the fire?
So he could sleep like a log.

What do you buy only to throw out?
Streamers.

What fish is also a poet?
An eel, because he is a Longfellow.

1ST MAN: Excuse me – why is your dog wearing black wellington boots?

2ND MAN: His brown ones are at the menders.

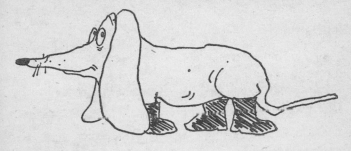

A man was sitting in the stalls of the cinema, moaning and groaning loudly. Eventually the usherette noticed him and asked him: 'What's your name?'

'Percy Pemble,' groaned the man.

'Where do you come from?'

'The balcony!'

A man met a scruffy old tramp who was only wearing one shoe.

'Hello, there!' said the man. 'Have you lost a shoe?'

The tramp replied, 'No. I found one.'

Why were pirates like contortionists?
Because they often sat on their chests.

Why did the man who walked three miles not get very far?
He only moved two feet.

JUDGE: So you and your wife have been fighting again. Liquor, I suppose?
MAN: No, your honour. She licked me this time.

What Scottish island would you have to look up to see?
Skye.

Why doesn't Sweden export cattle?
Because she wants to keep her Stockholm (stock home).

A wandering musician came into a village one Sunday morning. He stood outside the church, threw his hat on the ground, and fiddled away as the congregation filed out. With a stern look, the vicar went over to him.

'My man,' said the vicar. 'Do you know the Third Commandment?'

'I don't think I do,' said the fiddler. 'But if you whistle a few bars I'll soon get the hang of it!'

When is it impossible for a captain to write in his cabin?
When his hands are on deck.

What stands on one leg and has its heart in its head?
A cabbage.

Why did the Scotsman break a window?
Because he wanted to see glass go (Glasgow).

Why is getting up at four o'clock in the morning like a pig's tail?
Because it's twirly (too early).

What has four legs but isn't an animal, wears clothes but isn't a person, has feathers but isn't a bird?
A feather bed.

Why is a red-headed idiot like a biscuit?
Because he's a ginger-nut.

Games and Competitions

(*In which Cheating is Part of Winning*)

Some days you'll feel like playing games with friends and enemies. You'll want to compete; to see who's the champion riddle and joke teller. So here are a couple of sample games and competitions that will stimulate you in your quest:

Hunt the Riddle
For two players. Player A writes a riddle on a piece of paper and buries it in a haystack. Player B has to find it. The penalty for not finding it – having to listen to twenty jokes.

Mystery Joke Writers
For one player. While the school-teacher is out of the classroom, chalk a joke on the blackboard. The player who trembles the least when the teacher returns is the winner.

On which side of the head
is it best to wear a hat?
The outside.

A soldier and a sailor got into the car. Who was able to drive it?
The soldier, because he had the khaki (car key).

What tune does everyone like?
Fortune.

Why did the horse gallop over the hill?
Because he couldn't gallop under it.

CITY-DWELLER: Why do
  hens have such short
  legs?
FARMER: Because if they
  were taller, the eggs
  would smash with the
  fall.

I don't know what's the matter with me today,' muttered the centre-forward after missing an open goal. 'I'm not playing my usual game.'

'Oh?' said an opposing player with sarcasm. 'What game is that, then?'

What do trees do on January 1st every year?
Turn over a new leaf.

What can you say, and merely by doing so, break?
Silence.

Before the crowds had a chance to disperse after watching a Punch and Judy show, an evangelist began to lecture them:

'Can any of you children tell me what we must do before we can expect to have our sins forgiven?' he said.

'Yes,' replied a small boy. 'We must sin.'

What fish do you need if you're on ice?
Skate.

What ship would you take to a party?
An ice-breaker.

What can run swiftly without legs?
A mountain stream.

Why did the postman get
the sack?
To put all the letters in.

What are the best things to put in a currant cake?
Your teeth.

What can never ever be made right?
Your left ear.

Why is an elephant in a china shop like a house on fire?
Because the sooner they are put out, the better.

WOMAN: I'm having trouble with my husband. Every
  morning he washes the car.
DOCTOR: You should be proud of him. Most wives wish
  their husbands would wash the car more often.
WOMAN: In the *bath*?

How can you make a Maltese Cross with just one match?
Light it and stick it up his shirt.

When is a ship in love?
When she's attached to a buoy.

The big-game hunter came across a dinosaur in his travels.

'Hey, you're extinct!' he said.

The dinosaur was rather deaf: 'What was that you said?'

'You are extinct!' shouted the hunter.

'So would you be,' said the dinosaur, 'if you'd been dead for six million years!'

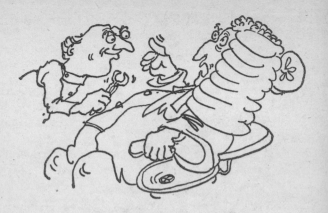

What did the judge say to the dentist?
Do you swear to pull the tooth, the whole tooth, and nothing but the tooth?

A holidaymaker who'd had too much to drink stood on the promenade. He gazed long at the reflection of the moon on the calm sea.

'What's that down there?' he asked a passer-by.

'It's the moon.'

'Well, how did I get up here, then?'

PATIENT: I keep losing my temper.
DOCTOR: I beg your pardon?
PATIENT: I've already told you once, you stupid, ignorant, deaf idiot!

Which game always has its ups and downs?
Snakes and ladders.

What do you need to see through a cement wall?
A window.

The weather had been very bad, and the blizzard disrupted all the traffic in town. Buses were snowbound, cars couldn't move. A telegram arrived for the manager of a shop:

'Will not be in to work today. Haven't arrived home yesterday yet. – Carruthers.'

How do you cope with a thirst at night?
Sleep on a mattress with springs in it.

Why should a batsman eat lots of spinach?
To make him strong enough to carry his bat for a century.

When is a ship's hold like a forest?
When it is full of trunks.

Why is a piano like the Royal Mint?
Because it makes notes.

What does a horse become after it's eight years old?
Nine years old.

A famous cricketer died and went to Heaven. St Peter
met him at the Pearly Gates.

'Who are you?' asked St Peter.

'I was a famous cricketer on earth.'

'Oh, good,' said St Peter. 'Nip back to earth and get
your bat – we're playing Hell tonight!'

The American tourist was looking over Russet's farm.

'How many acres have you got?' he asked.

'About fifty,' Russet said, with a proud smile.

'You know,' the American said. 'Back home in Texas
it takes me two days to drive around my ranch.'

'Poor you,' sympathised Russet. 'I had a car like that
once, but I got rid of it.'

CHEMIST: Did that mudpack I sold you last week help improve your wife's appearance?

GHERKIN: It did for a while. But then it fell off!

What, put in front of pies, makes them dangerous?
The letter S.

VICAR: I've been told you were drinking in a pub last Sunday instead of coming to church.

PARISHIONER: No, Vicar, that's not true – and what's more, I've a fine catch of fish to prove it.

What did the bride think when she arrived at the church?
Aisle, Altar, Hymn (I'll alter him).

1ST FARMER: What on earth are you giving to your chickens?

2ND FARMER: Boiling water.

1ST FARMER: Why?

2ND FARMER: I want them to lay hard-boiled eggs.

A policeman on his beat came across a street musician. Tapping him on the head with his truncheon, he said:

'Oy! Have you got a licence to play your guitar in the street?'

'Well, no, I haven't.'

'Then I must ask you to accompany me.'

'Certainly, Officer. What would you like to sing?'

PICKLES: I'm worried about my brother. He's been thinking for years that he's a hen.

DOCTOR: Good gracious. Why didn't you come to me before about this?

PICKLES: Well, we needed the eggs.

The foreman at the building site was very agitated.

'It's missing!' he shouted. 'It's missing! Every man on the site will have to be searched.'

'What's missing?' he was asked.

'The cement-mixer!'

What is the safest thing to do in a thunderstorm?
Catch a bus with a conductor.

When is a window nice to eat?
When it is jammed.

1ST MAN: That's a ridiculous pair of socks you're wearing – one's blue and the other's yellow.

2ND MAN: I know. And the funny thing is, I've got another pair at home exactly like these!

Riddles Without Any Answers

(For Quiz-Kids Who are Good at Running)

This curious-looking section is a challenge to your ingenuity. In it, you'll find lots of riddles – but the answers to the questions have purposely been left out. This is partly because there *aren't* any answers! Your job is to rack your brains to think of some suitable answers. If you can come up with a dozen answers in all, you're obviously some kind of genius.

Should you be unable to answer *any* of the questions, don't despair. For you can always bombard folk with an obscure riddle (such as 'Why is a banana-skin left-handed at night?'), then await their puzzled reactions as they try to think of the answer. When they eventually give up, adopt one of the two following courses:

(*a*) Reply, 'That's funny, I don't know either!' – and run away.

(*b*) Reply, 'Shan't tell you, so there!' – and run away.

Such a crazy game as this ought to provide endless, harmless amusement.

How many different directions has shredded wheat?

....

What did the manhole say to the pickled onion?

....

What's the difference between an inkwell and a rickshaw?

....

Why did the chicken cross the toad?

....

What did the chimney say to the brain surgeon?

....

What has eleven knees, five fireplaces, one hat, and a pint of lemonade in each ear?

....

Why do wardrobes tango in the middle of the night?

....

How many leaves are there on a sycamore tree?

....

Why did the toe-nail blush?

....

What did the log say to the Prime Minister?

....

What has a hundred bicycle pumps, no wheel, seven pairs of braces and can sneeze pop tunes?

....

Name two places where New Zealand has gone.

....

How many kidneys has a garden fork?

....

Which is the quickest way to eat motor-bikes?

....

What's the best place to look for a lost Cathedral?

....

Why do they put doughnuts into swimming-baths?

....

Riddles Without Questions

*(For Quiz-Kids Who Already
Know All the Answers)*

You've had riddles without answers – now have them
without questions! Impossible, you say? Probably you're
right. But it'll do no harm to give this revolutionary game
a try. Simply guess what the original question to the riddle
was. (Yes, they're *real* riddles this time: you can check up
at the end of the chapter, where a list of the original
questions to the riddles can be found. No peeking till
you've done the quiz, though!) Here's a ratings guide to
see how clever you were at guessing the questions:

15–20 correct: *Cheat!*

10–15 correct: *Cheat!*

2–10 correct: *Cheat!*

1 correct: *A brilliant effort.*

0 correct: *A bonus point for honesty.*

1. ....?

'Naturally, sir – it's been ground.'

2. ....?

Because peel follows peel.

3. ....?

'I can 'ear you.'

4. ....?

A boxing ring.

5. ....?

The star-fish.

6. ....?

Handshakes.

7. ....?

A matchstick.

8. ....?

When he cuts up a side street.

9. ....?

Chile.

10. ....?

A creeper.

11. ....?

No, it's taking.

12. ....?

'You might be board (bored), but I've been framed.'

13. ....?

They both curl up and die (dye).

14. ....?

Because it saw the zebra crossing.

15. ....?

Yes – a grocer sells salt and he can walk.

16. ....?

Buoys and gulls.

17. ....?

When it is bellowed at.

18. ....?

No, but April May before June.

19. ....?

Throw a clock over your shoulder.

Throw a clock over your shoulder

20. ....?

Shoe-trees.

Answers

1. What did the waiter say when the customer complained that the coffee tasted like mud?

2. Why are onions like church bells?

3. What did the sheaf of wheat say to the farmer?

4. What ring is square?

5. Who plays the leading part in 'The Underwater Opera'?

6. What shakes does everybody like?

7. What serves by being struck by its owner?

8. When is a boy in a hurry destructive?

9. What country must you wear warm clothing in?

10. What plant gives one a scare?

11. Is kleptomania catching?

12. What did the door say to the floor?

13. Why is a lady hairdresser like an autumn leaf?

14. Why did the bus stop?

15. Can a salt-cellar walk?

16. What children live in the sea?

17. When does a fire flare up?

18. Will February March?

19. How can you make time fly?

20. What trees have neither leaves nor bark?

The 1st, 2nd and 3rd Armada Books of Fun

compiled by Mary Danby

Butler: The invisible man's outside
Lord Prune: Tell him I can't see him

I sat next to the duchess at tea;
It was just as I feared it would be:
   Her rumblings abdominal
   Were simply phenomenal,
And everyone thought it was me!

Two hilarious helpings of ridiculous riddles, riotous
rhymes, crazy cartoons and preposterous puns, let
alone loony limericks and jokes by the score!

And you'll find all your favourite cartoon characters in
The 1st, 2nd and 3rd Armada Books of Cartoons

The Trickster's Handbook

200 tricks, jokes and stunts to fool your friends.

Peter Eldin

Instant Magic!
Astonish your friends in 200 hilarious ways.
Prove that 19 equals 20 . . . tear a telephone directory
in half . . . tell fortunes with a banana . . . float a
sausage in mid-air . . .

How's it done? Only you know, when you've got a
copy of The Trickster's Handbook. So keep it in a
secret place while you baffle your victims with
fiendish stunts and leg-pulls.

Another exciting Fun Book from Armada

Armada

The Armada Quiz and Puzzle Books

by Doris Dickens and Mary Danby

Boost your brain power and have hours of puzzling fun
solving the hundreds of different quizzes in this popular
Armada series.

Pick your favourite puzzle – names, pictures, anagrams,
codes, magic squares, pets, mysteries, sport, history,
spelling, doodles, and many, many more. Sharpen your
wits and get puzzling!

Have you discovered Armada's latest quiz books? Facts
and fun for everyone in some exciting titles:

Armada Horse & Pony Quiz Books
Armada Football Quiz Book
The Armada Animal Quiz Book
The Second Armada TV Quiz Book
The Great British Quiz Book
The Armada Round The World Quiz Book
The Zoo Quiz Book

Armada Science Fiction

Step into the strange world of Tomorrow with Armada's exciting science fiction series.

Armada Sci-Fi 1
Armada Sci-Fi 2
Armada Sci-Fi 3
Armada SF 4

Edited by Richard Davis

Four spine-chilling collections of thrilling tales of fantasy and adventure, specially written for Armada readers.

Read about . . . The monstrous Aliens at the bottom of the garden . . . A jungle planet inhabited by huge jellies . . . A robot with a human heart . . . The terrible, terrifying Trodes . . . A mad scientist and his captive space creatures . . . The deadly rainbow stones of Lapida . . . The last tyrannosaur on earth . . . and many more.

Stories to thrill you, stories to amuse you – and stories to give you sneaking shivers of doubt . . .

Begin your sci-fi library soon!

Armada

CAPTAIN ARMADA

has a whole shipload of exciting books for you

Armadas are chosen by children all over the world. They're designed to fit your pocket, and your pocket money too. They're colourful, gay, and there are hundreds of titles to choose from. Armada has something for everyone:

Mystery and adventure series to collect, with favourite characters and authors – like Alfred Hitchcock and The Three Investigators. The Hardy Boys. Young detective Nancy Drew. The intrepid Lone Piners. Biggles. The rascally William – and others.

Hair-raising spinechillers – ghost, monster and science fiction stories. Super craft books. Fascinating quiz and puzzle books. Lots of hilarious fun books. Many famous children's stories. Thrilling pony adventures. Popular school stories – and many more exciting titles which will all look wonderful on your bookshelf.

You can build up your own Armada collection – and new Armadas are published every month, so look out for the latest additions to the Captain's cargo.

If you'd like a complete, up-to-date list of Armada books, send a stamped, self-addressed envelope to:

Armada Books,
14 St James's Place,
London SW1A 1PF